HAL·LEONARD
INSTRUMENTAL PLAY-ALONG

AUDIO ACCESS INCLUDED

PLAYBACK+
Speed · Pitch · Balance · Loop

VIOLIN

IRISH FAVORITES

CONTENTS

To access audio visit:
www.halleonard.com/mylibrary

Enter Code
1166-7925-6433-5269

ISBN 978-1-4234-9531-4

HAL·LEONARD® CORPORATION

7777 W. BLUEMOUND RD. P.O. BOX 13819 MILWAUKEE, WI 53213

Visit Hal Leonard Online at
www.halleonard.com

BELIEVE ME, IF ALL THOSE ENDEARING YOUNG CHARMS

VIOLIN

Words and Music by
THOMAS MOORE

(rit. 2nd time)

THE BELLS OF ST. MARY'S

VIOLIN

Words by DOUGLAS FURBER
Music by A. EMMETT ADAMS

BLACK VELVET BAND

VIOLIN

Traditional

BRENNAN ON THE MOOR

VIOLIN

Traditional

COCKLES AND MUSSELS
(Molly Malone)

VIOLIN

Traditional

THE CROPPY BOY

VIOLIN

18th Century Irish Folksong

DANNY BOY

VIOLIN

Words by FREDERICK EDWARD WEATHERLY
Traditional Irish Folk Melody

EASY AND SLOW

VIOLIN

Traditional

THE FOGGY DEW

VIOLIN

Traditional

GREEN GROW THE RUSHES, O

VIOLIN

Traditional

THE HUMOUR IS ON ME NOW

VIOLIN

Traditional

I ONCE LOVED A LASS

VIOLIN

Traditional

I'LL TAKE YOU HOME AGAIN, KATHLEEN

VIOLIN

Words and Music by
THOMAS WESTENDORF

I'LL TELL ME MA

VIOLIN

Traditional

THE IRISH ROVER

VIOLIN

Traditional

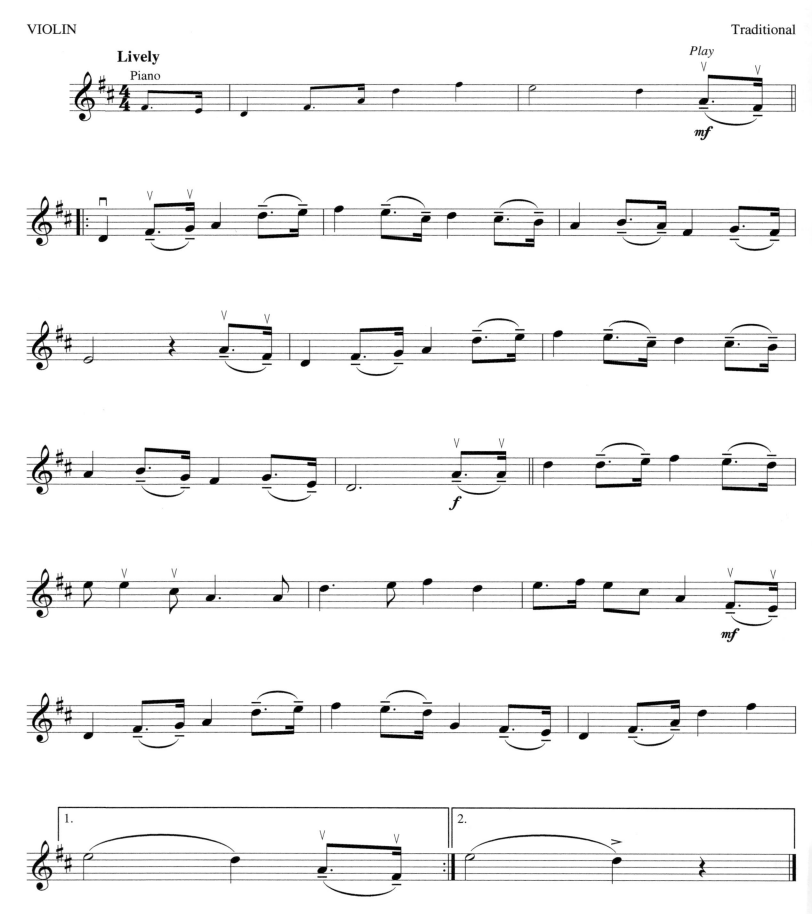

THE JOLLY BEGGARMAN

VIOLIN

Traditional

THE LITTLE BEGGARMAN

VIOLIN

Traditional

MacNAMARA'S BAND

VIOLIN

Words by JOHN J. STAMFORD
Music by SHAMUS O'CONNOR

MINSTREL BOY

VIOLIN

Traditional

MY WILD IRISH ROSE

VIOLIN

Words and Music by
CHAUNCEY OLCOTT

A NATION ONCE AGAIN

VIOLIN

Words and Music by
THOMAS DAVIS

THE OLD ORANGE FLUTE

VIOLIN

Traditional

THE PATRIOT GAME

VIOLIN

Traditional

RED IS THE ROSE

VIOLIN

Irish Folksong

THE RISING OF THE MOON

VIOLIN

Traditional

THE ROSE OF TRALEE

VIOLIN

Words by C. MORDAUNT SPENCER
Music by CHARLES W. GLOVER

TOO-RA-LOO-RA-LOO-RAL
(That's an Irish Lullabye)

VIOLIN

Words and Music by
JAMES R. SHANNON

THE WEARING OF THE GREEN

VIOLIN

18th Century Irish Folksong

WHEN IRISH EYES ARE SMILING

Words by CHAUNCEY OLCOTT
and GEORGE GRAFF, JR.
Music by ERNEST R. BALL

VIOLIN

THE WILD COLONIAL BOY

VIOLIN

Traditional

WILD ROVER

VIOLIN

Traditional